THE LIVING WORLD

HOW FISH SWIM

Jill Bailey

W
FRANKLIN WATTS
LONDON•SYDNEY

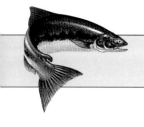

This edition first published in 2003 by
Franklin Watts
96 Leonard Street
London
EC2A 4XD

Franklin Watts Australia
45-51 Huntley Street
Alexandria
NSW 2015

ISBN: 0 7496 5149 0

A CIP catalogue reference for this book is available
from the British Library.

© Marshall Cavendish Corporation, 1997, 2003

Series created by Discovery Books Ltd.
Originally published as *Nature's Mysteries: How Fish Swim*
by Marshall Cavendish Corporation,
99 White Plains Road, Tarrytown, NY, 10591, USA.

Printed in Malaysia

Acknowledgments
Illustrated by Colin Newman
The publishers would like to thank the following for their permission to reproduce photographs: cover David B.
Fleetham/Oxford Scientific Films, title page Carl Roessler/Bruce Coleman, 4 Howard Hall/Oxford Scientific Films,
5 top Michael Pitts/Survival Anglia/Oxford Scientific Films, 5 bottom & 6 Jane Burton/Bruce Coleman, 8 Peter
Scoones/Planet Earth Pictures, 10 Michael Glover/Bruce Coleman, 11 Carl Roessler/Bruce Coleman, 12 Neville
Zell/Oxford Scientific Films, 13 top Max Gibbs/Oxford Scientific Films, 13 bottom Carl Roessler/Bruce Coleman,
14 Marty Snyderman/Planet Earth Pictures, 15 top Peter David/Planet Earth Pictures, 15 bottom Peter Parks/Oxford
Scientific Films, 17 Fritz Prenzel/Bruce Coleman, 18 Max Gibbs/Oxford Scientific Films, 19 Georgette Douwma/Planet
Earth Pictures, 20–21 Jeff Foott Productions/Bruce Coleman, 22 Peter David/Planet Earth Pictures, 24 Charles & Sandra
Hood/Bruce Coleman, 25 Jane Burton/Bruce Coleman, 26 Richard & Julia Kemp/Survival Anglia/Oxford Scientific
Films, 27 top Howard Hall/Oxford Scientific Films, 27 bottom Jane Burton/Bruce Coleman, 28 Charles & Sandra
Hood/Bruce Coleman, 29 Marty Snyderman/Planet Earth Pictures

(Cover) Sweepers swim together in a shoal for safety. Predators find it hard to pick out an individual from the glittering mass of fish.

CONTENTS

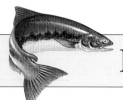

DIFFERENT STROKES

The fastest fish in the sea, the sailfish, can swim faster than a cheetah can run. The basking shark, which may be four times as long as the sailfish, does not swim nearly so fast. Why is there this difference?

Fish require different swimming skills for different needs. The sailfish is a hunter, chasing schools of fast-swimming fish and spearing them with its pointed snout. The basking shark is a filter feeder; it cruises slowly along the surface, taking in water through special gills to filter out millions of floating microscopic creatures.

Fish such as tuna often need to travel very long distances in search of food. They must be able to swim fast for long periods of time.

The sailfish can reach speeds of up to 109 kilometres per hour (68 miles per hour). When swimming fast, it folds the large sail-shaped fin on its back into a special groove to make its body more streamlined.

▲ *Moray eels wriggle into narrow crevices where they lie in wait for passing prey, putting on a powerful burst of speed when their dinner comes within reach.*

Sea horses live in shallow water close to the shore, and do not need to swim far or fast. When they swim, they do so "standing up," waving their side fins to propel themselves along.

▶ *Sea horses must avoid being swept into deep water. Instead of using their tail for swimming, they coil it around weeds to anchor themselves.*

GETTING UP SPEED

When you swim, you can feel the energy it takes to push your body through water. Water is around eight hundred times denser than air so it takes much more effort to move through it. As you push water away behind you, you move forward in the water. The force that propels you forward is called thrust.

Waves of bending pass along the bodies of eels as they swim. As an eel wiggles its body, it pushes the water away behind it and to either side, which makes the eel move forward.

The red arrows show the direction in which the water is being pushed. The large blue arrow shows the direction in which the fish is moving. The small green arrows show the sideways and backward thrust at different places on the fish's body.

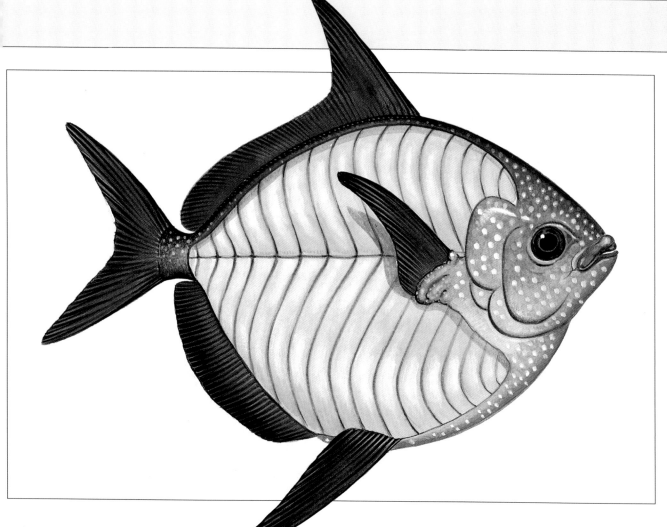

The simplest way for a fish to swim is to bend its body from side to side. If you watch an eel swim, you'll notice that waves of bending pass along its body: Each part of the body bends first to the right, then to the left. As the eel bends, the water is pushed backward and sideways, producing forward and sideways thrust. Since the body bends equally to the right and the left, the sideways thrusts cancel each other out, and the eel moves forward on a straight course.

A fish's muscles are arranged in zigzag-shaped blocks along its sides. Opposite blocks of muscles work against each other; when muscles on one side pull tight (contract), the muscles opposite relax so the fish's body bends to the side where the muscles are contracting.

A fish's skeleton is ideal for bending. Its vertebrae — the individual bones in its backbone — can move relative to each other at the joints when they are pulled upon by muscles. A fish's muscles may make up over half its body weight.

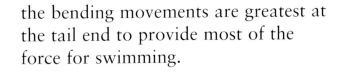

Most fish are more or less streamlined, or torpedo shaped. A torpedo is roughly oval in shape, wider at the head than at the tail. This shape provides the least resistance to water as the fish moves forward. Since the head end of a fish is fatter and less flexible than the tail, the bending movements are greatest at the tail end to provide most of the force for swimming.

For most fish, fins are also important for steering, braking, and often propelling. Fins are fan-shaped webs of skin supported by rays of bone or cartilage. Each ray has its own set of muscles. Just as in the main body of the fish, waves of contraction and relaxation pass along the muscles of the fin rays. They swing the fin, propelling the fish along. These waves can pass in either direction so they can be used for braking as well as for going forward.

Sea goldfish swimming among corals on a reef show how different fins can be raised and lowered, twisted and turned. A fish's streamlined shape helps it push through the water. The main push when swimming comes from the tail, while fins are used for balancing, steering, and braking. The large fish in the centre is using its tail fin as a rudder as it turns to the left.

There are two kinds of fish skeletons. Most fish have a bony skeleton (top). Small bony struts, called rays, support the fins but are not attached to the main skeleton. Each ray is moved by its own set of muscles. Sharks, skates, rays, and lampreys have a skeleton made of softer material called cartilage (bottom).

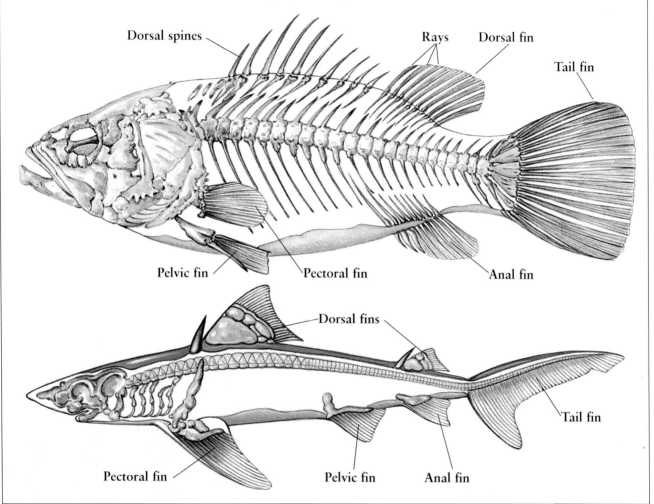

There are two main sorts of fins — paired and unpaired. The vertical unpaired fins on the fish's back and belly (the dorsal and anal fins) and the tail fin help to keep the fish stable in the water, preventing it from rolling over to one side. The tail fin is also used for steering. The paired fins (the pectoral and pelvic fins) keep the fish horizontal, with its head and tail at the same level in the water, and can also be used to brake and back paddle. By changing the angle of the paired fins, the fish can rise or sink in the water.

SWIMMING WITH STYLE

Really fast-moving fish rely mainly on their tails, which may provide up to 90 percent of their swimming power. They also have rather special muscles. If you eat fish, you probably have noticed that the flesh of a salmon or mackerel is much darker and redder than the flesh of a cod. This is due to special red muscles that are able to store much more oxygen to provide energy for swimming.

By using different fins to different degrees, each kind of fish has evolved its own unique way of swimming. Shoals of sea goldfish twist and turn rapidly, while barracuda speed forward like flying needles. Shrimpfish hover head down among the spines of

Hundreds of silverside fish wheel and twist together around a lone diver at the edge of a coral reef. Keeping together helps protect them from enemies.

sea urchins for camouflage. The pike, which stays motionless for long periods waiting to ambush small fish, has very delicate flexible fins that it uses for fine control to keep itself in exactly the same position, regardless of water movements.

Skates and rays flap their huge pectoral fins up and down rather like wings to fly through the water; they use their tails only for steering. Their pectoral fins have another use —

Lionfish have stiff, spiny fin rays tipped with poison for defence. They advertise this fact with bright warning colours.

when the ray comes to rest on the sea floor, it uses these fins to flick sand over its back until it's almost buried, hidden from the eyes of predators. Gurnards display large colourful fins when courting or defending territory. Gouramis have long, threadlike pelvic fins, which they use as feelers in murky water; they also use these fins to stroke their mates.

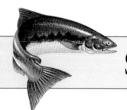

SHAPE AND STYLE

Sharks are fatter — and heavier — at the head of their body than at the tail. A simple thrust from their tail could easily send them head down into the ocean depths. To compensate for this, the shark's two pectoral fins are spread horizontally at such an angle that they generate an upward thrust, called lift. These fins are fairly stiff so the shark does not need to spend much energy keeping them at the correct angle. But this means that it cannot bend them quickly to brake. If a shark meets an unexpected obstacle, it can only try to swerve out of the way.

The giant manta ray swims near the surface. Its huge wings, up to 6.5 metres across, enable it to glide almost effortlessly through the water as it filters shoals of tiny fish and crustaceans through its wide mouth.

The boxfish has such a stiff body that it cannot bend. It has to rely on its fins to propel it along.

The wide pectoral fins of rays and skates avoid the lift problem of the sharks but are less effective for swimming. These fish usually cruise slowly near the seabed, feeding on shellfish living in the mud.

Boxfish and sea horses have such stiff armour on their bodies that they cannot bend them. Instead, they use their paired pectoral fins for swimming.

▲ The triggerfish swims using mainly its dorsal and anal fins, which are very close to the tail. The front of the body is almost free of fins so the fish can nose into crevices in the reef in search of food.

13

SWIM OR SINK

The basking shark drifts at the surface of the ocean as it feeds on tiny plankton, yet it may weigh up to eight tonnes. How does it do it? Water is much denser than air and can support animals much better. Even so, an object will float naturally only if its body is less dense than water. But the bodies of fish are usually denser than water; a fish must reduce its density if it wants to avoid sinking. In addition, as a fish goes deeper in the ocean, the water becomes colder and denser, and the pressure of the water above it increases dramatically. A fish must change its density as it changes depth.

Fish have several ways of solving this body density and water pressure problem. Some simply keep swimming, using their fins to provide lift. If a shark or a dogfish stops swimming, it sinks.

The great white shark weighs over 3.3 tonnes. Its liver weighs more than 450 kilograms and contains a great deal of oil, which helps keep it afloat. Even so, if the shark stops swimming, it will sink.

▲ *Lantern fish spend the daytime deep in the ocean but travel up thousands of feet to shallower water to hunt at night. Nobody knows how they cope with the density and pressure problems of this change in depth.*

Some sharks also store large amounts of oils in their body. Oils are less dense than water so their presence reduces the overall density of fish. Some oils change density with temperature, thus helping fish adapt to changes in depth. A few sharks have large oily livers. In some shark species, 30 percent of the body volume and 80 percent of the liver itself may be made up of oil. Many sharks used to be hunted for their oil.

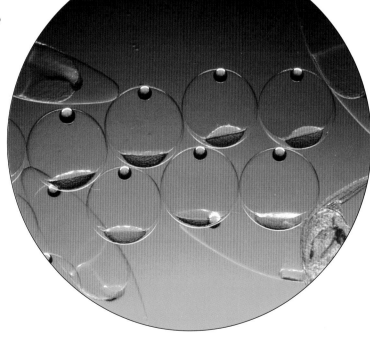

Fish eggs and baby fish that live in water near the surface often contain oil droplets to keep them afloat.

STAYING STEADY

Many fish have gas-filled swim bladders, lunglike sacs filled with gas, usually nitrogen and oxygen, the main gases found in air. The gas reduces the fish's density, and the outward pressure of the gas helps counteract the pressure of the water above the fish. These sacs probably evolved from the lungs used by ancient fish living in stagnant waters to gain extra oxygen from the air. Some primitive fish still have a tube linking their swim bladder to their throat; they can refill the bladder with air at the water's surface. Most fish, however, have a closed swim bladder.

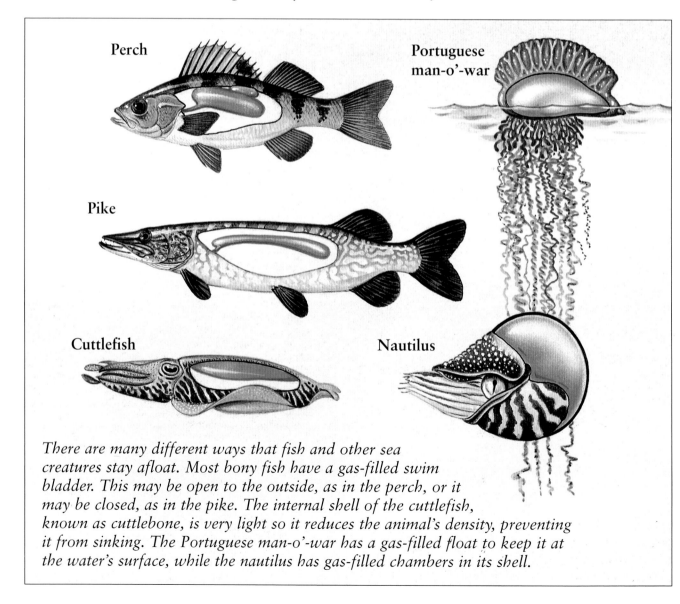

Perch

Portuguese man-o'-war

Pike

Cuttlefish

Nautilus

There are many different ways that fish and other sea creatures stay afloat. Most bony fish have a gas-filled swim bladder. This may be open to the outside, as in the perch, or it may be closed, as in the pike. The internal shell of the cuttlefish, known as cuttlebone, is very light so it reduces the animal's density, preventing it from sinking. The Portuguese man-o'-war has a gas-filled float to keep it at the water's surface, while the nautilus has gas-filled chambers in its shell.

Mackerel and tuna, which swim nonstop at high speeds, have no swim bladders. Like sharks, they must keep swimming to avoid sinking.

The volume of the swim bladder and the pressure of the gas inside it can be adjusted to balance the outside water pressure and density so the fish remains at a constant depth. If the fish wants to change depth, it must absorb or secrete gas into the swim bladder.

The swim bladders of some fish have other uses as well. In over five thousand species, the bladders are linked to the fish's inner ears and are used as amplifiers for receiving sound vibrations. Some fish have special

Some of the sounds fish make with their swim bladders can be very loud: The toadfish's underwater calls reach an intensity similar to the noise of a subway train!

drumming muscles attached to the wall of their swim bladder, which can be used to produce a variety of sounds, from thumps and groans to clucks and barks. Some fish — grunts, drumfish, and croakers — are named for their sound-producing skills.

Weather loaches are sensitive to changes in air pressure. Their swim bladders are used like lungs in the stagnant water they live in. If atmospheric pressure falls before a storm, the fish are disturbed and let out air, acting as living barometers.

FLYING WITH FINS

As you sail through the tropics, groups of fish leap out of the water and glide through the air, diving back in only to emerge again a few seconds later. These are flying fish. They use their large winglike pectoral fins for gliding. To take off, the flying

The main purpose of fish flight is to escape from predators, but sometimes the predator can also fly. Dolphin fish will hurl themselves out of the water to chase gliding prey or skim just below the surface to catch it when it reenters the water.

▲ *Flapping their transparent "wings" like birds, hatchet fish are quite capable of leaping out of an aquarium. If they have a long enough takeoff run, they can fly about three metres through the air.*

fish accelerates toward the surface at up to thirty kilometres per hour (twenty miles per hour), then, flicking its muscular tail up to fifty times a second, it leaps into the air and spreads its "wings".

A few fish really fly more like birds, flapping their wings. Barely 6.5 centimetres long, the tiny hatchet fish of tropical rivers in Central and South America, and the butterflyfish of western Africa, seem unlikely candidates for flight. Although their bodies are deep and flattened, specially fused bones in their chest and shoulders provide strong attachments for flight muscles that work on the large pectoral fins.

▼ *Flying fish can glide for up to 40 metres and, aided by air currents, may rise to a height of 9 metres. They sometimes land on the decks of ships.*

▲ *Weighing over 700 kilograms, a marlin is a powerful acrobat – the ultimate challenge to a fisherman. When hooked, it will leap many times into the air and can sometimes throw off a hook.*

DOING THE SIDE STROKE

Flatfish spend most of their lives on the seabed, swimming lazily in search of shellfish and crustaceans or burying themselves in the sand or mud to rest. When they swim, they look as if they are bending their bodies up and down, but, in fact, they are really bending them from side to side — flatfish swim on their sides.

A baby flatfish looks just like any other baby fish, but as it gets bigger, it begins to swim on one side. The lowermost eye moves around its body to lie alongside the upper one, and the mouth also twists. If you look closely at a flounder, you can see it has a twisted face. The fins on the back and belly are now stretched out horizontally. The fish swims by bending its body up and down. At each stroke, the water is pushed backward and up or down. The up and down thrusts cancel each other out so the fish moves forward.

The life story of the flounder — how an ordinary little fish turns into a flatfish.

   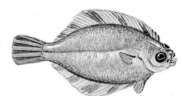

As the baby flounder grows, its mouth twists and one eye moves around the body to lie alongside the other eye.

Dolphins — which are not fish but marine mammals — bend their bodies up and down. So do porpoises and the great whales. But in these animals almost all of the thrust is produced by the tail end of the body and by the tail flukes, which are horizontal.

21

DEEP-SEA DIVING

Life in the very deep ocean calls for some very special adaptations. Fish living 4,000 metres or more below the surface experience extremely high pressures. This pressure tends to squash a fish's body, making it more dense. The water at this depth is also very cold, not much above freezing, and there is no light. Only about half the species living below 200 metres have swim bladders; if they do, the swim bladders are very large to counter the great weight of the water pressing from above.

The more water a fish contains, the less dense it is. Many deep-sea fish have very watery flesh and are flabby to the touch. They often have weak skeletons, weak muscles, and no scales, which also reduces weight. The weak skeleton and muscles mean that these fish cannot swim very fast, but to try to swim fast under such immense

This anglerfish lives deep in the ocean, where there is no light. It does not have to swim fast to catch its prey. A wormlike structure on its forehead with a light-producing tip lures prey within reach of its huge mouth.

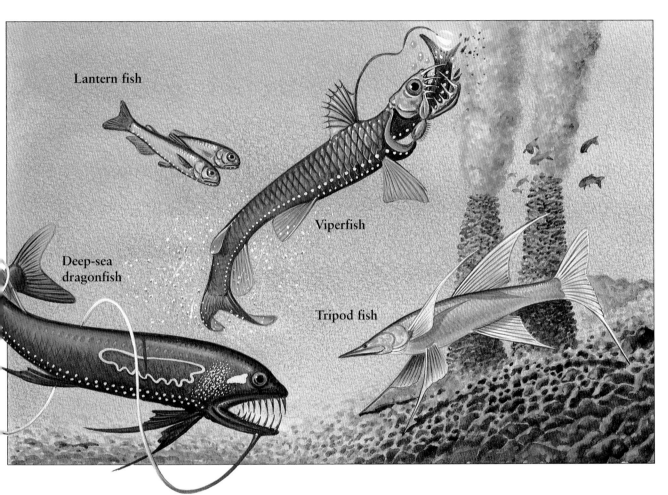

Lantern fish

Viperfish

Deep-sea dragonfish

Tripod fish

pressures would use up a great deal of energy. Since the food to provide this energy tends to be sparse in the ocean depths, speed is impossible.

With no light, fish have to rely on touch and on sensing vibrations in the water to find their food. The tripod fish, which lives on the deep-sea floor, has long stiff tips on its pelvic fins and a long stiff tail fin. These form a natural tripod for propping the fish up above the muddy water next to the

Deep below the ocean surface, there is almost no light. Many fish have light-producing organs that act as camouflage; from below, the lights hide the fish's dark outlines. Some fish, like the viperfish, use luminous lures to attract their prey. Because food is scarce, many deep-sea fish can open their mouths very wide to seize large prey. The tripod fish lives on the deep ocean floor, using its long pelvic and tail fins to prop itself up as it searches for food.

sea floor. It can even walk gingerly on these stilts or hop along, using the tripod to land on.

SWIMMING ON DRY LAND

Catfish have been called the walking, talking fish. Their swim bladders amplify both incoming and outgoing sound vibrations. Some species can even survive for short periods out of water, using their swim bladder or gill chambers to store oxygen. They can travel overland by bending their body to and fro, pushing against stones and other small bumps in the ground instead of against water, and using their stiff pectoral fins as stubby legs. If the pool they're staying in dries up they can move to another one. Eels are also famous for their overland journeys, sometimes of a mile (1.5 kilometres) or more. They manage this by moving in much the same way as snakes.

Blennies and gobies rest on the seabed on their stiff pelvic fins. They may come out of the sea and hop from rock to rock at low tide, storing air and water in their gill chambers.

The batfish looks rather like a frog with a tail. It has bulging eyes and a large mouth. Its pectoral fins form stumpy little legs, and its pelvic fins are shaped like a frog's hind legs, helping to take its weight.

The mudskippers of mangrove swamps can stay out of water for quite a long time by absorbing air through the moist lining of their mouth and throat. They flick themselves over the shore by digging their tail fin into the mud, then suddenly flexing it. The pectoral fins' rays bunch together to form struts, rather like a pair of crutches, while the pelvic fins take the fish's weight.

Male mudskippers flick their dorsal fin (the one on their back) up and down to make a threatening display when challenging other males — and showing off to females. Each fish defends a small territory on the mud.

Mudskippers can even climb the mangroves' aerial roots to get away from predators. The bases of the pelvic fins join together to form a small sucker that helps them grip vertical surfaces.

ROWING AND KICKING

Many other kinds of animal can swim. Like fish, large swimming animals are usually streamlined. Dolphins and porpoises are clearly torpedo shaped; otters have small flat ears to reduce the water's drag against their head and they hold their legs close to their bodies when they swim.

Webbed feet work rather like fins — by spreading the toes instead of the fin rays, the owner can stretch out its web to give a large surface to push against the water. You see this very clearly if you watch a frog swim. Many different animals have webbed feet, including otters, ducks, sea gulls, crocodiles, and alligators. The flippers of seals, sea lions, walruses, and whales are much stiffer than webbed feet, but they can turn through a wide angle in several directions.

The goosander is a fish-eating duck that pursues its prey under water. By stretching out its long neck and folding its wings close to its body, this bird can take on a streamlined shape. It rows with its webbed feet to propel itself through the water.

◀ *Sea lions are graceful underwater acrobats. Their streamlined bodies are very flexible, and they propel themselves with their webbed hind flippers. They use their front flippers for steering and braking.*

▼ *A water beetle rows itself along under water using its large hind legs. Bristles on its legs help to increase the surface area pushing against the water.*

Crustaceans and water insects have flat legs, fringed with stiff bristlelike hairs that increase their legs' surface area. On the legs of water beetles and backswimmers these hairs are hinged at the base so they can be spread out during the power stroke and laid flat against the legs on the return stroke. Swimming crabs also have large flattened legs, which act like paddles.

Most of these animals use a rowing action to swim. Their legs or webbed feet enter the water at an angle to reduce resistance, then turn to a vertical position for the push stroke, returning to the angle for the recovery part of the stroke.

Turtles cannot bend their bodies, nor can they spread out their feet. They use a different method for moving through the water — their flattened legs act as hydrofoils. A hydrofoil is like an aircraft wing in cross section; it is streamlined and curved on the underside so water passing over the upper and lower surfaces is at different pressures. This produces lift. Penguins appear to "fly" underwater. This is not far from the truth — instead of acting as airfoils, their wings act as hydrofoils.

Octopus, squid, and cuttlefish have a quite different way of moving, especially when they want to make a quick getaway. They use jet propulsion. Water stored in their body cavity is expelled by powerful muscles, shooting the animal in the opposite direction.

The green turtle travels thousands of miles across the ocean when it migrates to its breeding grounds. It uses its flattened flippers like hydrofoils to keep from sinking.

Squid and cuttlefish have highly streamlined bodies, while the octopus can squeeze its body into a streamlined shape, stretching out its tentacles and holding them close together like a tapered tail. If threatened by a starfish, scallops will take to the water, clapping their shells together to expel water and jet propel themselves out of harm's way.

Fish have been evolving their swimming skills for at least 500 million years. Today, there are almost 21,000 different species of fish swimming in every way imaginable. Some are able to move about under

When it swims, the octopus squeezes its body into a more streamlined shape. When it is moving extremely fast by jet propulsion, it will straighten out its tentacles and hold them even closer to its body.

the immense pressure of the deep ocean, while others speed along the surface or even glide through the air above it. The shape and size of a fish's body and the position and arrangement of its fins are adapted to its mode of swimming. This great adaptability has allowed fish to lead different lives, from filtering plankton and grazing on algae and corals to hunting and eating fish and other marine animals.

GLOSSARY

airfoil: the shape of a wing that causes the air flowing past it to be at different pressures above and below, producing lift.

algae: very simple plants that live in water. Most are tiny, but a few large ones we know as seaweeds.

cartilage: a rubbery substance, softer than bone, out of which the skeletons of sharks, skates, and rays are made.

crustacean: a kind of animal with a soft body and a hard outer shell, living mostly in water. Crabs and lobsters are crustaceans.

density: the weight of something in relation to its size (volume).

display: a special kind of behaviour used by an animal in courtship, mating, and defending territory.

hydrofoil: the shape of the fins of fish, the flippers of turtles and seals, and the wings of penguins that causes the water flowing past them to be at different pressures above and below, producing lift.

jet propulsion: moving forward by shooting out jets of water or air backwards.

lift: the upward push that is produced by a fin or a wing.

plankton: tiny animals and plants that live in the surface waters of the sea.

rays: supports made of bone or cartilage that keep fins in shape.

stagnant: water that is still and contains very little dissolved oxygen.

streamlined: having a smooth torpedo shape that gives little resistance when moving through water or air.

water pressure: the pressure water places on an object beneath it. The deeper the object is, the more water there is above it and the greater the water pressure.

webbed feet: feet that have sheets of skin and tissue stretched between the toes, giving the feet a greater surface area.

USEFUL WEBSITES

To find out more about how fish swim, visit some of the websites listed below. You can also use them to explore other aspects of the living world, and to get involved in nature events across Britain and Australia.

To find out more about strange sea creatures, visit **www.sealife.co.uk**. This is a fun and up-to-date interactive site which also gives information about sealife centres across Britain.

For information on individual fish, visit the Yahooligans' fish web directory at **www.yahooligans.com/content/animals/fishes**. You'll find a huge list of fish to choose from, each one accompanied by great photographs and an easy-to-read fact file.

The 'Cool Science for Curious Kids' website at **www.hhmi.org/coolscience** is a fantastic interactive site covering a wide range of science topics.

The Young People's Trust for the Environment is a charity which helps children and young adults explore and understand the environment. The website at **www.yptenc.org.uk** gives up-to-date reports on environmental issues. You will also find lots of ideas on how to get involved in environmental work and events.

Channel 4's excellent educational website provides students and teachers with all the essentials. For help with tricky topics like microorganisms or how things move, visit **www.channel4.com/weblogic/essentials/science/life/index.jsp**

The children's BBC wildlife website at **www.bbc.co.uk/cbbc/wild** is a fun and informative site, with easy links to other educational wildlife sites.

To explore Australia's vast and varied natural environment visit **www.ea.gov.au/education/activities**. This site includes great quizzes, games and activities for children, as well as teaching support materials for teachers.

Note to parents and teachers

Every effort has been made by the Publishers to ensure that these websites are suitable for children; that they are of the highest educational value, and that they contain no inappropriate or offensive material.

However, because of the nature of the Internet, it is impossible to guarantee that the contents of these sites will not be altered. We strongly advise that Internet access is supervised by a responsible adult.

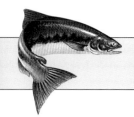

INDEX

Numbers in *italic* indicate pictures